MW01145232

The Volatility of the Options Market

Adapting Your Strategy to Market Conditions

Elijah Williams

Copyright 2022. All Rights Reserved.

This document provides exact and reliable information regarding the topic and issues covered. The publication is sold with the idea that the publisher is not required to render accounting, officially permitted, or otherwise qualified services. If advice is necessary, legal or professional, a practiced individual in the profession should be ordered.

From a Declaration of Principles which was accepted and approved equally by a Committee of the American Bar Association and a Committee of Publishers and Associations.

In no way is it legal to reproduce, duplicate, or transmit any part of this document in either electronic means or printed format. Recording of this publication is strictly prohibited, and any storage of this document is not allowed unless with written permission from the publisher. All rights reserved.

The information provided herein is stated to be

truthful and consistent. Any liability, in terms of inattention or otherwise, by any usage or abuse of any policies, processes, or Instructions contained within is the solitary and utter responsibility of the recipient reader. Under no circumstances will any legal obligation or blame be held against the publisher for reparation, damages, or monetary loss due to the information herein, either directly or indirectly.

Respective authors own all copyrights not held by the publisher.

The information herein is offered for informational purposes solely and is universal as such. The presentation of the data is without a contract or any guarantee assurance.

TABLE OF CONTENTS

Chapter 1. Risk Management

Quantitative and Qualitative

Risk management is both qualitative and quantitative. The quantitative bit is far easier to understand since it is just a matter of crunching numbers and monitoring a bunch of statistics with regards to your account. Now, if you were trading directionally, the number of metrics you need to monitor is enormous.

Thankfully, when it comes to options, you only need to track a few. Let's take a look at these.

Risk per Trade

More than anything else, it is your risk per trade that determines your success. Common wisdom is not to risk more than two percent of your capital per trade and in the case of options trading, this is correct. Directional trading requires you to risk far less than this in order to be successful.

The true measure of a good trader is how consistent they are in risking the same percentage of their account on each and every trade. A lot of beginners get on a winning streak at times and then start playing loose with this, only to be hit by a big loss that wipes out all their prior gains.

There is a school of thought that proposes that risking a fixed amount per trade, as opposed to a fixed percentage, is a better model. Suffice to say that, risking the same amount will bring you greater gains per trade and exaggerate your winning streaks but will do the same to your losses.

What's more, thanks to your losses being exaggerated, you'll have to keep making more and more gains to simply breakeven constantly and this will wipe out your account pretty soon since the basic math of all this is against you. Remember, you can't precisely predict the outcome of most trades in advance. Thus, it's best to risk the same percentage of your account every trade.

Win Percent

The win percentage of your strategy, that is the number of times you make money, is one half of an important measure that determines whether you'll make money or not. Usually, thanks to the way we've been brought up and have had UR performances measured in school, we chase the highest win percentages, thinking ninety percent is better than forty.

Well, in academia, this is true. However, in the chaotic world of the markets, this is far from the case. Making money on a trade is not about being right. You can be right about the markets and still lose money in the long run. This is best explained after we look at the second half of the equation.

Average Win Percent

Your average win percent is the amount of money you win on average, when you do make money, expressed as a percentage of your account or as a multiple of the amount you risk per trade on average. So, if you risk R per trade, which might be 2% of your account, and if you make 4% on a win on average, you will make 2R per win.

The average win percent and the win percent together determine whether you'll make money or not. So out of ten trades, if you win two, a win rate of twenty percent, and your average win is 2R, you will not make money. This is because your eight losses will cost you 8R and your wins will only amount to 4R. This is a net loss of 4R.

However, if you make 5R on average per win, you will make money with a twenty percent win rate. In this case, your losses will add up to 8R as previously, but your wins will add up to 10R, giving you an overall profit of 2R. If you risk two percent of your account, this is a profit of 4% over ten trades.

Now if you manage to take two hundred trades over the course of a year, you'll be making 80% in a year. This is precisely what professional traders do make and it takes an extraordinarily high level of skill to hit such numbers. My point is that your profitability is determined by both numbers, not just a single one.

As you can see, it is perfectly possible to make money by being 'right' just twenty percent of the time. In a regular academic examination, this will guarantee your failure, but in the markets, it's just one half of an equation.

Strategy Evaluation

This gives us an excellent method of figuring

out the profitability of strategies. If a strategy has a low win percent but high average win percent, it is perfectly valid to implement it, instead of trying to chase strategies that have high win percentages simply. For example, if you have the previously described strategy and another one with a 90%-win rate but only a 0.5R average win percent.

Over two hundred trades, the previous strategy makes 80% but this strategy, which is correct 90% of the time, will make you 35% over the same number of trades. So, which is the better strategy? The one where you have more losses or the one where you have more wins? Clearly, asking which one has more wins or loses is missing the point.

So, don't blindly chase high win rates or strategies that claim you won't lose even a single trade. For the rest of us, evaluating both the win percentage and the average win size as a function of the percent risk per trade is what determines whether or not a strategy is good.

Qualitative Risk

Let's say you settle down in front of your television on the weekend and switch on the TV to catch your favorite game. You're fully prepped and have your TV and assorted accessories set just so. Your friends have come over as well and all in all, it's a great atmosphere. There's just one problem: your team's star athlete, the one on whom the result of the game hinges, has turned up to the game hungover.

Now, it isn't unheard of such things to happen in pro sports, but when it does happen, you can imagine the reaction that follows. The athlete is roundly criticized as a buffoon, rightly so, and the sports media have a field day debating where he's about to be traded to next. We instinctively understand that preparation is the key to success and turning up hungover is hardly good preparation.

Yet, how many of us sit down to trade after having just walked in from work? We're tired and frustrated from whatever is going on in that world and think we can simply waltz in and make money in the markets. The very same markets that are full of professionals who make a living from it and are responsible for the management of many millions and billions.

Do you seriously think anyone can be successful trading this way? Do you think trading is simply a matter of learning the right strategies and then implementing it with the snap of a finger? If so, this is an indicator that your mindset is incorrect and that you don't understand what trading risk management involves.

Make no mistake; you will need to prepare and have your wits fully about you as you sit down to trade. You cannot afford any distractions like checking your smartphone or trying to wing something at the last minute. You need good sleep and need to exercise and eat well.

This is why I called the adrenaline-filled, coked-out atmosphere of trading floors in movies unrealistic because it is impossible to trade this way. A lot of beginners get seduced by this 'devil may care' type of depiction and try to do the same when it comes to their own hard-earned money. Needless to say, this results in a quick wipeout and the ones who will take their money are the traders who have prepared themselves.

You need to follow a specific mental and physical routine prior to operating in the markets. Meditation and other mental calming techniques are a great idea and will enable you to see things clearly, as they are. Also, avoid trading when things are not going well for you with your regular life.

There's no rule that says you have to trade each and every day of the year. Take adequate time to reflect on your skills and practice them well. Practice them so well that you know them by heart. The live market is not a place for you to be questioning whether the signal is valid or not. You simply need to pull the trigger and execute.

Sometimes, despite our best intentions, we fail to follow our plans. This is an indication that the problem is not so much with our technical strategy or risk but with our mindset.

Option Trader's Mindset

Options trading is most suitable for a certain personality type and mindset. But if you are intrigued by the concept of options, but you simply have not had a chance to develop the correct mindset before, there are a few tips that we can rely on to get in the right frame of mind.

You Can Weather the Storm

Options prices can move a lot throughout short periods. So, someone who likes to see their money protected and not losing any is not going to be suitable for options trading. Now, we all want to come out ahead, so I am not saying that you have to be happy about losing money to be an options trader. What you have to be willing to do is calmly observe your options losing money, and then be ready to stick it out to see gains return in the future. This is akin to riding a real roller coaster, but it is a financial roller coaster. Options do not slowly appreciate the way a Warren Buffett investor would hope to see. Options move big on a percentage basis, and they move fast. If you are trading multiple contracts at once, you might see yourself losing $500 and then earning $500 over a matter of a few hours. In this sense, although most options traders are not "day traders" technically speaking, you will be better off if you have a little bit of a day trading mindset.

You Don't Make Emotional Decisions

Since options are, by their nature, volatile, and very volatile for many stocks, coming to options trading and being emotional about it is not a good way to approach your trading. If you are emotional, you are going to exit your trades at the wrong time in 75% of cases. You don't want to make any sudden moves when it comes to trading options. As we have said, you should have a trading plan with rules on exiting your positions, stick to those rules and you should be fine.

Be a Little Bit Math-oriented

To understand options trading and be successful, you cannot be shy about numbers. Options trading is a numbers game. That doesn't mean you have to drive over to the nearest university and get a statistics degree. But if you do understand probability and statistics, you are going to be a better options trader. Frankly, it's hard to see how you can be a good options trader without having a mind for numbers. Some math is at the core of options trading and you cannot get around it.

You are Market-focused

You don't have to set up a day trading office with ten computer screens so you can be tracking everything by the moment, but if you are hoping to set up a trade and lazily come back to check it three days earlier, that isn't going to work with options trading. You do need to be checking your trades a few times a day. You also need to be keeping up with the latest financial and economic news, and you need to keep up with any news directly related to the companies you invest in or any news that could impact those companies. If the news does come out, you are going to need to make decisions if it's news that isn't going to be favorable to your positions. Also, you need to be checking the charts periodically, so you have an idea of where things are heading for now.

Focus on a Trading Style

As you can see, there are many different ways that you can trade options. In my opinion, sticking to one or two strategies is the best way to approach options trading. I started off buying call options, but now, I focus on selling put credit spreads and iron condors. You should pick what you like best and also something that aligns with your goals. I moved into selling put credit spreads and iron condors because I became interested in the idea of making a living from options trading with regular income payments, rather than continuing to buy calls and hope that the share price would go up. There is no right or wrong answer, pick the trading style that is best suited to your style and needs.

Keep Detailed Trading Journals

It's easy to fool yourself when trading options, especially if you are a beginner. I hate to make the analogy, but this is kind of like going to the casino. If you have friends that gamble at casinos, then you are going to notice that they tend to remember the wins, and they will forget all the times that they gambled and lost. I had a cousin that won a boat, and she was always bragging about how she won a boat at the casino. I remember telling her that yes, she won a boat, but she paid $65,000 more than the boat was worth to the casino over the years. You don't want to get in the same situation with your options trading. It can be an emotional experience because trading options are active and fast-paced. When you have a profitable trade, it will be exciting. But you need to keep a journal to record all of your trades, to know exactly what the real situation is. That doesn't mean you quit if you look at your journal and find out you have a losing record, what you do is figure out why your trades aren't profitable and then make adjustments.

Options Traders are Flexible

I have said this before, but one thing you need to remember about options trading is you can make money no matter what happens to the stock. So, you need to avoid falling into the trap of only trading options to make money one way. Most frequently, people do what they have been brainwashed to do and they will trade call options hoping to profit from rising share prices. If you are in that mindset now, you need to challenge yourself and begin trading in different ways so that you can experience making money from declining stock prices, or in the case of iron condors, stock prices that don't even change at all. You need to be able to adapt to changing market conditions to profit as an options trader. So, don't entrap yourself by only using one method. Earlier, I said to use one or two styles, but you should be ready to branch out when market conditions change. Remember this – market conditions always change eventually. As I am writing, we are in the midst of a long-term bull market, but it won't last forever.

Take a Disciplined Approach

Don't just buy options for a certain stock because it feels good. You need to research your stocks. That will include doing fundamental analysis. This is going to mean paying attention to the history of a stock, knowing what the typical ranges are for, stock in recent history is, and also reading through the company's financial statements and prospectus. Remember, I suggest picking three companies to trade options on for a year and also two index funds. The index funds require less research, but for the three companies that you pick, you should get to know those companies inside and out. Stick with them for a year, at the end of each year, evaluate each company. Then decide if you want to keep them and bring them forward into the following year's trades. If one company is not working out for you, then move on and try a different company.

Trading with LEAPS

Leaps are interesting options. They expire a year or more into the future. This is different than the short-term options that most people are trading. LEAPS are more expensive, but they can also represent money-making opportunities. LEAPS also give you an indirect way to control stock.

Profiting from LEAPS

LEAPS have high prices because they have a lot of extrinsic value. Looking at June 18, 2021, Facebook call options, the $195 call is priced at $42.13 a share. So that represents a $4,213 options contract. According to the chart, it made 3.4% today, which isn't a huge amount, but I challenge you to find a bank or mutual fund that has a return of 3.4% per day. The open interest is 133. This meets our minimum criteria for getting involved in a trade. It's quite small compared to Facebook options that expire in the following month, but it's enough open interest that it's going to be possible to get in and out of a trade in a reasonable amount of time. The implied volatility is a solid 33%. For comparison, the $195 call that expires in three weeks is priced at $12.48.

Although LEAPS are expensive, they have a lot of potential for profits. You can get into a LEAP and if the stock makes a solid move, you can close your position and make large amounts of money. For that $195 call that expires in June 2021, the delta is 0.64. That means that even though the option has a lot of extrinsic value since it expires a long way into the future, it's pretty sensitive to price changes in the stock that is with the option. If the share price goes up to $1, the option price will go up by $64. LEAPS don't suffer much from time decay. Theta for this option is only 0.03. If the share price goes up to $20 after an earnings call, the option is going to go up by $1,280. So, you can make pretty good profits. The barrier to entry is the high price to buy one.

Poor Mans Covered Call

One of the interesting things that you can do with a LEAP is you can use it to sell covered calls.

That sounds crazy, but it works. You can use the LEAP to cover call options that you sell to open. So, you can invest in LEAPS at a fraction of what it costs to invest in the stock, and then start selling calls against the options to generate income. Although it might cost $4,600 to buy a Facebook LEAP, it would cost nearly $20,000 to buy 100 shares of stock. Buying a LEAP gives you de facto control over a hundred shares of stock at a much smaller price than the investment cost.

For the price of 100 shares of Facebook, you could invest in 4-5 LEAPS, and have a lot more room to work with as far as selling call options. So, you could end up having a higher income.

Chapter 2. Designing a Trading Plan Flexibility: Adapting Your Strategy to Market Conditions

The trader must never be obstinate, he must agree to adopt. This situation is obviously delicate. A good trader must rigorously apply his trading plan, while not considering the rules of the plan as immutable. Traders often apply the same strategy regardless of market configuration. The good trader considers the different market conditions and develops the most effective strategies for each situation. Thus, some day-traders have a strategy for opening, another for mid-day and finally one for closing. Others have adopted specific strategies for bull markets, bear markets and for trend-free markets. A good trader is able to adapt to changing markets and new conditions.

In addition, market conditions change over time (the market of the 2000s is different from that of the 1990s). Some effective strategies have not been effective today.

Nevertheless, the adaptation of the strategy must be based on in-depth research work and a critique of the methods used. The trader should never question his system when operating in real-time because it can be harmful. This phase of reflection should always be conducted calmly: the trader must prioritize strategic thinking before the fight and apply his strategy calmly in the heat of the moment.

Finally, for the great trader Mark Weinstein, "no approach in technical analysis works all the time. You have to know when to use each method. I do not believe in mathematical systems that approach markets in the same way. I use my person as the system and I constantly change the input to achieve the same output: profit."

The professional trader is constantly adapting its strategies to market conditions. He questions his system and tries to improve it with the aim of performance. Some principles are immutable, but it is still possible to improve certain rules or techniques of opening and closing positions, and this is what the big trader should be trying to do by being flexible and adapting himself to the evolution of the market.

Look For the Line of Least Resistance

The strategy must always stick to market circumstances. The trader must know the direction of the flows because it is by marrying that he dominates them. In trading, you should never oppose the course of things and respect the famous saying "trout is your ally". We must leave the market to dictate the procedure to follow and not pretend to want to impose our certainty.

Thus, when a market is without trend, it is dangerous to apply a trend tracking strategy. In this case, the trader will only have to buy support and sell resistance. The trader must pierce the intentions of his opponents, the object of the analysis. He must decipher the intentions of professional traders, including detecting the right signals and eliminating false signals.

Lessons Learned

A successful trader lets his profits run and quickly cuts his losses. As a result, it maximizes profits and minimizes losses and achieves gains on average greater than losses.

In low-performing traders, the average loss is usually greater than the average gain: they quickly exit their winning positions and return to hope mode when the market invalidates their point of view instead of facing reality. Everything seems linked: the successful trader has a high payoff ratio and an honorable probability of success, which allows him to take more risks and thus to record a superior performance.

Example of a Trading System

Suppose that the trader relies on the following criteria to open a position:

- To position himself only in the presence of a double-bottomed graphic figure;

- Bullish divergence on the validated RSI, - MACD higher than its signal line.

The trader has tested his system over quite a long history, and he finds that it has a probability of success of 60% and a payoff ratio of 2. It is a profitable system that can be used in the markets. Nevertheless, the probability of success, as well as the payoff ratio, is based on past data, which the trader will never know for sure if they will happen again. The only thing he can handle is a risk, which proves the importance of money management.

Vary The Size Of Its Positions?

Some traders use the same size regardless of the market configuration. They consider equiprobable events and believe that each configuration must, therefore, be assigned the same risk capital. This approach does not seem optimal for us and we think that it is necessary to vary the size of the position according to the opportunity that presents itself: to increase the size of its position when the opportunity seems excellent and its potential still important; reduce the size of the opportunity does not really give satisfaction, or even completely out of it.

It should be noted that novice traders do the opposite: at the outset, they allocate the same risk to all opportunities (good or bad); after a series of gains or losses, they increase the size of the position, whatever the opportunity, and take significant risks. They are suffering new losses that push them to engage more and more transactions, but also to increase the size of their positions, which can sometimes lead to ruin.

The performance relies heavily on the trader's ability to vary the size of his exposure based on opportunities. Likewise, it involves taking bigger risks and accepting higher drawdowns. Despite this, we remain convinced that good traders take much less risk than others and remain cautious in their decisions, even if they are not afraid to take positions. They consider that without risk-taking there are no possible gains.

This point of view was also defended by Thorp in his famous book Beat the dealer, which discusses the importance of increasing one's risk when probabilities are in our favor. Nevertheless, he also insists that conditions only favor 10% of the time and that it is during this period that we must maximize our chances of success. The payoff ratio must be favored over the probability of success.

Many traders place a lot of importance on the probability of success because it means that they are often more right than wrong. In fact, the payoff ratio has much more weight than the probability of success.

The payoff ratio is often low for traders because of the psychological bias highlighted by Kahneman and Tversky. In fact, individuals have a much greater aversion for losses than the satisfaction gained from the gains made: a loss is twice as painful as the satisfaction gained from a gain of the same amount. It is for this reason that people tend to take profits very quickly and not take their losses (so not to execute their stops) or even to ignore any information about them because they seem too painful.

Chapter 3. Options Definition and Function

Apart from the popular financial instruments available on the market today such as stocks and bonds, there are other instruments known as derivatives.

A derivative refers to a financial instrument that gets

its value from other instruments or assets. One example of these derivatives would be options.

By definition, options are financial instruments derived from an underlying asset such as stocks or bonds. They present you with an opportunity to purchase an underlying security at a specific date and price. In other words, options represent contracts that allow you to buy and sell a certain value of an underlying asset at a particular price. Each contract specifies certain terms about the trade.

How Do They Work?

Options provide you with a very reliable way of investing in stock trading. Just like any other financial transaction, an options agreement or contract is made up of two people—a buyer and a seller.

An individual contract represents a number of shares of the underlying security. In most cases, one contract covers 100 shares of stock. The buyer always pays a certain amount against each contract as the premium fee. This amount is always determined by the type of underlying asset as well as the option strike price.

Traders often use options as a form of investment because of the limited number of risks involved in these derivatives. This is because options enable people to protect their real stocks from financial market exposure. However, care must be taken when dealing with options since, like any other trade, it is very easy to lose a large amount of stock within a fraction of time. They involve high profits, but may also result in high risks if not handled well. Despite this, many people consider options as one of the best and most reliable financial instruments on the stock market.

Options as Derivatives

As stated earlier, options are not real stock. They are derivatives whose price is determined by the price of the underlying security. Other examples of derivatives include futures, swaps, forwards, calls, and puts among several others.

Since options only represent a certain asset, the contract entered by a buyer and seller only offers you the ability to trade on the options market. An option call gives you the right to purchase an underlying security at a specific cost and time whereas a put option grants you the capability to sell on the market at a specified period of time and cost. Each option transaction represents two sides—the buying side and the selling side.

Selling of an option is also known as writing an option. Each side of an option transaction involves its own rewards and risks. When a person buys an option, it is said that they have obtained a long position; when they sell an option, they have a short position. This applies to both call and put transactions.

In options trading, asset owners do not get involved in the transaction. Cash is only exchanged between the parties involved in the options transactions. Most of these transactions happen between investors, brokers, and market makers.

Chapter 4. Types of Options

Options come in two major types—put options and call options. Traders choose the kind of option to trade-in depending on whether they want to buy or sell on the options market.

Call Options

The call option options make it possible for you to purchase an underlying asset associated with the option in question. When a call option is in the money, the bid or strike price is less in value than the underlying stockprice. Traders always buy a call option when there is a possibility of its stock price to increase beyond the current bid price before the expiration is obtained. When this happens, the trader derives some profit from the call transaction. Individuals who purchase call options are always known as holders. Once they acquire the option, they can sell it any time before the expiration date. The profit of any option is obtained by subtracting the strike price, premium, and transaction fees from the stock price. The resulting amount is what is called the intrinsic value. This difference is always a negative value when the trader has made a loss and zero value when no profit or loss has been realized. The maximum amount that a trader can lose from an option is equivalent to its premium. This explains why most people purchase options and not the underlying security.

The call option comprises three components—the strike price, the premium, and the exercise or expiration date. The premium is the amount of money that a trader pays when acquiring a particular option. For instance, a trader may purchase a call option with $55 as the strike price, a $5 premium, and an expiration period of one month; it means that you will pay the seller $5 as the premium. If the expiration date is reached before you exercise the option, you will only pay the $5. If let's say, a week later the price goes up to $70 and you decide to sell your option, you will make a profit of $15 from the transaction less $5 paid as the premium. If the price goes below

$55, you make a loss.

Investors may also decide to sell a call option when

they are anticipating a decline in the stock price. As the stock price falls to a level that is lowerthan the strike price, the investor will get some profit from the transaction. The person selling a call is known as the writer of the call. They must sell shares to a buyer at a price determined beforehand.

Put Options

This grants you the ability to write or sell an asset or security at a cost thatis already predetermined, also the expiration date. Both call and put options can be used on stocks, commodities, currencies, and indexes as underlying securities. In this case, the strike price becomes the cost by which you sell the option.

A put option allows you to sell a certain asset at a known cost and expiration date. This option can be used on a good number of underlying assets including indexes, currencies, commodities, and stocks. The price at which a trader sells an option is called the strike price.

Traders make a profit from selling a put option when anticipating a decline in the strike price. They make a loss when the value of the stock increasesto a level that is beyond the strike price. This indicates that the cost of a put option may rise or fall as time elapses.

The intrinsic value of a put option can be derived by obtaining the difference in the prices of the stock and the option. The resultant valuekeeps changing as the time value reduces in strength. When a stock option bears a positive intrinsic value, you say that it is in the money. A negative value of this shows that the option has fallen out of the money.

Similar to call options, you do not need to wait for your put options toexpire before you exercise them. Since the premium value of an option continues to vary with the price of the shares or the cost of any other underlying asset, you must exercise your options just at the right time to avoid incurring losses in the future.

Options and Stocks

If you have been keen enough then you must have realized that moreinvestors are joining the options market more than the stock market. Stock trading has for a long time been the most popular form of trading on financial markets. You may be wondering if indeed options trading is better than stock trading. One great aspect of options is that they allow you to do more than just trading. Options have several characteristics that cannot be found in other financial instruments. One such characteristic is the use of Greeks, which are mathematical figures that help estimate the risk associated with each option. Traders can use these figures to avoid some trades that seem too risky.

There are several other differences between options and stocks. When you purchase shares of stock from a certain company, you acquire ownership of the percentage of the company. This means that you can sell off the shares anytime you wish to do so.

On the other hand, options do not grant you ownership of stocks. They only represent derivatives of the company stocks that are traded on certain predefined terms.

The main reason why investors purchase stocks is to sell them later when the price goes high. They, therefore, wait for the value of a certain stock to decline before making a purchase, then again wait for the price to go up in order to sell the same. When it comes to options, investors use them as a way of generating income and not necessarily as a form of investment. Options traders are never interested in the underlying stock. Most of them trade on short-term engagements. This is why the options market is always filled with almost all kinds of traders.

The trader relies on certain changes in the performance of the option to make money.

Another clear difference between stocks and options is the issue of time. Stocks can be traded for as long as decades. They do not have an expiration period. Once you invest in the stock market, it may take you as little as a few days to as much as several years to close your positions and make a profit. However, this can only happen when the company issuing the shares continues to exist. This privilege is missing in the options market since eachoption has a specific date of expiration.

Most people who invest in stocks always end up with good profits in the long-term. This is because m ost companies that sell shares keep building their brand portfolio, making it impossible for them to collapse. As the company grows, the share value grows as well. When it comes to options, the value a trader receives at the end of each transaction is very uncertain. Options trading is somehow likened to gambling, which may end in a winor loss.

Each trade involves a number of aspects that determine the outcome. It is upon the trader to understand these aspects and apply them accurately in order to realize a profit. Ignoring the rules of trade always results in a loss.

Another great difference between stocks and options is that stocks arealways sold in the form of preferred stocks or common stocks while optionsare traded in the form of contracts. Common stocks are those that cover a percentage of the participation in the profit of the company while preferred stocks are those that pay dividends to the investor. Traders receive these dividends at predefined intervals and amounts. Options contracts, on the other hand, serve as agreements between the buyer and the seller based on certain terms that both have to agree upon.

The pricing of stocks and options also differs.

The value of each stock sharedepends on how the company performs in the long-run, as well as some market factors. On the other hand, the cost of options is determined by an array of factors such as time decay, expiration date as well as the value of the underlying security.

In terms of risk, a stock trader only risks losing their capital if the company underperforms or stops operating. This means that if the company continues to operate, the trader is sure of getting most of their capital back with some profit. In options, the highest value that a trader can lose is equivalent to the amount of capital invested in each position. Since there is an unlimited potential of losing the premium, it means that options trading involves morerisk than stock trading. It may take years for a stock investor to lose part of their capital; however, it takes a matter of minutes or hours for an options trader to lose their premium.

Chapter 5. The Options Contract

An options contract is an agreement providing you with the authority or right to acquire or give out an asset for a specific amount of money. Basically, an options contract represents 100 shares of stock.

Each contract is defined by two categories of people—buyers and sellers. To purchase or sell options, the involved parties must fulfill the rules or formalities stipulated in the contract. In some cases, cash is used to settle contracts instead of shares.

For every contract, the person buying or acquiring a purchase position is the holder, and the seller is known as the writer. An option that is not exercised during the stipulated timeframe expires at the end of this period. One good thing with options is that the loss is often deducted from the money you put in as capital. Once an option expires, you can no longer engage in transactions based on the underlying stock.

The payoff pattern for stocks is almost similar to the one used in stock trading. The contract acts as a form of leverage for each transaction. This is because the holder or writer of each contract only gets control of a small percentage of the underlying security.

This means that traders only get the rights to a tiny portion relating to the stock being traded.

During each transaction, businesspeople can keep reinvesting their profits into the same position until the option expires. This gives the trader good leverage during price fluctuations. It is always easy for a trader to exercise an option before its value starts to diminish. This is one way of minimizing the risk of losing all the premium invested in the market. Options contract provide several details about the market and the trade. Justlike any other trade, you are required to make some payment before you tart trading. Each contract is governed by a number of terms definedbelow:

Derivative

We have defined options as forms of other instruments. This is a contract between traders with a value that is dictated by the value of underlying security. For each contract that involves derivatives, involved parties must first agree on the initial cost of the underlying asset. Options are considered derivatives since they only give you the right over a percentage of certain commodities.

Strike Price

This describes the cost or value of an option at any particular time. The strike price can also be referred to as the agreed-upon price. It is the cost of an option agreed upon by the buyer and the seller when making an options contract.

In the case of a call option, the strike price is the value placed as the cost a trader pays to gain rights around the underlying stock. In terms of the put option, the strike price generally implies the cost about which the seller relinquishes the rights to security.

This price does not change during the period of the contract. It is notaffected by any market and stock elements. Strike prices are some of the determinants of the profit one can make from the market. If underlyingstock prices rise beyond the amount of the strike price, one of the thingsthat will rise is the cost of the option and this is the best time for sellers to close their positions at a profit. When the value of the stock drops below thestrike price, buyers can purchase options at this point with the hope that the same price will rise. When there is a variation in regards to the strike price and with relations to the price of the market, this variation is what will beused to calculate the profit.

Expiration

What expiration means is a period when a given options get to an end.When the exercise date is attained, it means that it is no longer available for trading. The difference between the start and end dates of an option is known as its time period.

The value of an option often decreases as it approaches the expiration date. In most cases, this date can range from afew hours, days, or even years.

The Underlying Security

This is the asset used to define an options contract. It is the underlying stockupon which you trade your options. It is an essential component of the options market since it enables you to come up with the price and risks associated with certain stocks. It also allows you to choose the right options with the highest profit potential. In most cases, the cost of any option is determined using the worth of the underlying security.

Share

Shares are units of stock belonging to a certain company. Each option represents 100 shares of stock.

Contract Size

The contract size is the number of shares or stocks represented by a given option contract.

For example, if a contract covers 100 shares, then 100 isthe contract size.

The Premium

We have mentioned this severally before. The premium is the price you need to pay in order to acquire rights on an option. The premium can also be defined as the income that you receive from selling or writing an optionscontract. It can also refer to the cost of a given contract before it expires. In most cases, the premium is quoted in terms of dollars per share. The premium highlights a combination of three components—the time component, intrinsic component, and implied volatility of the asset.

Traders obtain the intrinsic value from calculations based on subtracting the asset cost from the strike cost. In a call option, this amount is equivalent to the current cost of the stock or security less the strike price. In the case of a put option, this value equals the amount set as the strike price minus the cost of the current stock.

When it comes to the options trading business, what is known as the time value comprises the amount a trader is willing to pay, with the hope that market prices will change in their favor. This time value drops when the option approaches the exercise date. Basically, how much more time is available before the expiration of an option, the higher its time value. When more time is available, it is easy for investors to pay more premium for the option with the hope that its price will change in the future. When there is less time until the expiration of an option, more traders will shy away from investing in the option since very little price change is expected.

The premium, therefore, is an addition between the option time value and the intrinsic value of the option.

Chapter 6. Options Trading

Most people always think of the stock market when they want to invest. Actually, a good number of stock market traders do not understand what options trading is all about. Stock trading has several benefits; however, it may not work for individuals who wish to invest on a short-term basis. Long-term investment strategies such as the buy and hold can help investors increase their wealth significantly, however such strategies do not provide better profits like some short-term ones. This is where more active short- term methods like options trading come in. These are often characterized by more returns.

Options trading has continued to become more and more popular. Basically, it involves the trading of financial derivatives known as options. The concept of options trading is not new. The first options contract was made in 1973 at an Exchange in the Chicago Board. There is a lot of similarity between the options traded today and those used at that time. However, a lot of things have changed in terms of the market size, trading terms, and the volume of exchange carried out every single day. People invest in options for various reasons, which will be discussed later in this chapter.

Options trading is a great way of investing money. Both the wealthy and average people can invest in the business since it does not require a lot of capital to start. Like we mentioned earlier, options are contracts that work within specific time limits.

Trading styles for options do differ from one region to another. This means that options can be categorized as American, European, Barrier, Bermudan, or Exotic options among several others. When trading options, you must be able to tell the style involved to enjoy the necessary gains. American options, for instance, close at the end of every third Friday of the month of expiry. The price of an option on this date becomes the closing price for the position. One major characteristic of American options is that you can close any moment between start and exercise days. European options, on the other hand, must be exercised on the date of expiration and not before. Positions for these options close on the third Thursday of the expiration month. There are also barrier options, which can only be exercised after the stock value rises beyond a certain level.

Bermudan ones are to be closed anywhere between start and exercise dates while exotic options make use of non-standard exercise procedures.

What Is Involved in Options Trading?

Basically, options trading involves the buying and selling of options contracts in the options market. Traders make a profit by purchasing contracts at relatively low costs and selling the same at higher costs.

When you buy a call option, it is like you are betting that the share pricewill rise in the future. For instance, if you purchase a call option for company X for $1500, you are indicating your certainty that the cost of the asset will shoot upwards beyond this purchase price for you to make aprofit. Every time you purchase a put option, you are anticipating a decline in the cost of the underlying security. In stock market terms, you are expecting a bearish outcome on the stock.

Options trading is more flexible than stock trading. This is because options are derived from a wide array of underlying securities. This gives traders more variety in terms of the scope involved in the trade. Investors use the price of options to determine price movements of stocks, commodities, foreign currencies, and indices.

This presents a lot of profit-making opportunities that may not be present in the stock market. More versatilityis also realized in the numerous types of options and orders that traders can place on the market.

Stock traders only have two ways through which they can make a profit— that is long positions and short positions. However, in options trading, investors get spoilt for choice since positions can be executed in several diverse ways and combinations.

Purchasing Options

Purchasing an options contract is just similar to purchasing stock. Investors buy options by selecting what they wish to buy, stating the amount then placing a buy to open order either directly or indirectly through a broker. If he value of the option goes up, you can sell it or exercise it depending on what works for you. One serious advantage of options trading is that youcan make money from price increases and also from price declines. If you anticipate a rise in the prices, you can buy a call option and if you anticipatea drop in the prices, you can purchase a put option.

When you decide to buy an option, you will get several contracts on the same underlying stock. This will be in terms of the types of calls and puts available for the same stock. For instance, you may find an option for company selling at $100 for each share, and find several others for the samecompany selling at different premiums.

Buying a Call Option

Let us assume that you want to purchase a call option for company A with an exercise cost of $60, a premium of $10, and an expiration date of one month. 7 days later, the stock price increases to $75. This means that you will make some $15 from the transaction. However, since you had already paid a premium of $10 to place the order, your profit will be $15 less $10 which comes to $5.

This is as illustrated below.

Figure 1: Buying a Call

If the price of stock declines to, say, $50 per share and you decide to let the option expire on its own. You will get an outlay of -$10, which is equivalentto the premium you paid for the order.

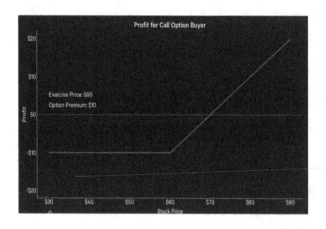

Buying a Put Option

Let us also assume that you are purchasing a put option from company Afor $45, a premium rate of $15, and an expiration of one month. After one week, the price drops from $45 to $25. If you exercise the option at this point, you will get a difference of $20. Your profit at their point will be $20less than the premium that is $5.

Selling Options

Writing or selling of contracts occurs in two ways. The first one is whenyou have pre-bought contracts that you want to release at a profit; similarly,in a position when you do not want to suffer more losses, then you canplace a sell to close order on the options market. You can raise this order if the price of the option has gone up and you want to get some profit fromthis change, or if the option price is constantly falling and you want to closethe position before you incur more losses.

The second way is throughopening short positions. This is what is known as the writing of options because the strategy involves creating new contracts for the options market.When a buyer agrees to your contract, you will be obliged to sell the underlying security associated with the contract to them.

The process of writing options is often completed using the sell to open order. The seller receives a payment that is equivalent to the strike price as soon as they place this order. Using such orders may sometimes be riskier than engaging in ordinary buying and selling, but it may also come with higher returns in terms of profit. Most investors place the sell-to-open order when they are certain that the buyer will not close a contract early enoughas they seek to generate some income.

Selling Calls

This involves allowing the buyer to make purchases against an asset or underlying equity. The market prices and other factors may force a seller to give away some equity with the price agreed on earlier as the strike price.

When the investor selling a call option also turns out to be the one owning the underlying equity, the process gets the name "writing a covered call." If the person selling the same option turns out not to be the one owning the stock, then the process gets referred to as "writing a naked call."

Selling a Put Option

Besides buying put options, you may also sell them at a profit. Investors who sell put options do so with the hope that the options will lose value in the future. When a trader sells a put option to the buyer, they have some authority to acquire the equity involved in the trade at a predefined cost if the option is exercised. For the seller to make a profit, the cost of the equity should remain either as it is or goes higher beyond the current strike cost. In case the cost remains under the strike cost, the involved seller makes a loss while the buyer makes a profit from the trade.

When it comes to options trading, profit is made from selling, buying, and writing options, not necessarily by exercising them. The point at which a trader exercises a contract depends on the strategies used in the trade aswell as the need to acquire underlying security. This means that you can make a profit both from exercising options and from just buying and sellingthem.

Expiration

One aspect that governs options is their expiration capability. At the end of each expiration period, the trader realizes a profit or loss. The reason why most traders try to learn and apply as many strategies as possible to each trade is that they want to realize profits for each contract. Most traders always feel frustrated when a contract ends without yielding any profit.

The profit of an option is determined by its intrinsic as well as time value. This is why it is important to consider the expiration period of any contract before investing in it. Some options may seem promising in terms of profitsbut end up at a loss because of the short expiration period. Options also do exist only for the period of time that the underlying stock is available on themarket for trading. Once a company stops listing its stock on the market,the options related to this particular stock will cease to trade as well.

The more an investor holds onto options, the more its value decreases. Unlike stocks, options tend to expire faster, and as the expiration date nears, the possibility of making profits from the trade also diminishes. Professional traders always ensure that they get more out of an open contract before it gets too late.

Chapter 7. The Volatility of the Options Market

In the options market, the term volatility describes the way the cost of a specific equity fluctuates over a period of time. Highly volatile options are often derived from highly volatile stocks; these carry more risks. Options with low volatility are always a featureless risk. In the options market, those stocks that feature high volatility always cost more than those with low volatility. It is not easy to identify certain stocks in terms of their volatility levels since it is easier for some low volatility stocks to become highly volatile and vice versa. Volatility is of two types—implied or historic.

The historical type of volatility is alternatively called statistical volatility. It measures price fluctuations based on predetermined time frames. It helps you to determine how the price of a particular option fluctuates over a period of time, say one year. A rise in historical volatility increases the cost of the equity in question. When this amount drops, the price of equity also goes back to normal. By understanding the changes in options prices over time, investors can make informed decisions on when and how to invest in a particular type of option. For instance, if the historical volatility of a particular option for 6 months is 25% and the volatility over the last 5 days is 50% it means that the stock has a volatility that is higher than normal.

Implied volatility, on the other hand, refers to the estimation of a particular stock or future volatility of the option based on some market factors. It is also known as projected volatility and is mostly used by traders who wantto determine the future prices of certain options. This type of volatility is often derived from the cost of a given option. Traders make use of the price as well as the historical performance of an option to determine its future price trends.

In case you are purchasing an option that has a high potential to generate profit, the premium of such an option may be higher than other options. This is because you can easily sell the option at a profit. Such positions are claimed to be in the money. Another trade may be "at the money" indicatingthat the cost is similar to the price of the equity.

There is another one that can get "out of the money," which means that the cost of trading the option is way higher than the value of the equity. An option like this one is not good since it is almost impossible for you to get some profit from it.

Once a call option gets in the money, it indicates that the cost of the equity has shot higher than the strike cost. When a put option gets in the money, the cost of the underlying equity is far below the strike cost.

If there is still a wide time gap between the beginning and end of a trade transaction, more time is available for a trader to make a profit.

Chapter 8. Benefits of Options Trading

One major reason why people invest in options is the level of risk involved and the returns realized. By now, you must have noticed the huge difference between trading with options and trading directly with stocks. Options can be traded in combination with other financial instruments to leverage profits. The trade is easily carried out and, in most cases, the profits are very good.

Options are considered by many people as a great alternative to stock trading. They do not cost much and help secure your underlying assets during the trade. Let us look at some of the major advantages that options have over other investment tools.

Options Involve Lower Costs

We have already mentioned the fact that options have a high potential for generating large profits for small capital investments. Most people trade-in options as an alternative to other forms of investment for this particular reason. Even those with very little capital can gain significant profit from the trade so long as they apply the right knowledge and strategies.

This means that traders can open an option position with the same potential as a stock position using lower amounts of capital. Let us say for example, that you wish to purchase 100 shares of stock at $80 for each share. This means that you will need to raise $8000 to make this purchase. However, if you were to buy the same shares using two call options, each with a premium of $20, then you will need half of the total capital for the same value of the stock. This is because each call represents 100 shares. Two calls will represent 200 shares, multiplying this by $20 per share comes to $4000.

The low costs of trading options are quite advantageous because they give investors the potential to raise large amounts of income over a short period of time. This advantage is absent in a number of financial instruments, especially those that are long-term since large amounts of cash must be invested in such instruments to generate income.

Options Are Associated with Reduced Risk Levels

Each financial investment tool bears a number of risks and this also applies to options trading. For most of these tools, it is always assumed that the higher the risk, the higher the returns. However, this is not true with optionssince there is a high balance between the risk and reward of each transaction. On most occasions, the risk of a trade is very little compared to the reward realized. Some market factors make it possible for traders to make a profit at very low risks. One great advantage of the options marketis that you get to choose the kind of strategy you want to use in your transactions by first determining the amount of risk you are willing toexpose your investment. You can always balance various strategies and market factors to balance or lower the risk involved in each position. The more you understand the basics of options trading, the more you will know how to minimize the risks involved in the trade.

The success of each trade always depends on the trader's ability to mitigate risks. If you do not understand how to measure risks and work around them, it may be difficult for you to generate profit from some transactions. Although there is still a high risk of losing your capital when trading options, this risk is relatively low compared to the risk of trading stocks or underlying securities. The only amount you may lose from trading options is the premium amount. If you analyze your contracts correctly and stick to the rules of trade all the way, you will always make some profit from options trading.

The strategies used in assessing options help investors to calculate the risk involved in certain contracts before putting their money in any of these contracts. This makes it easy for traders to estimate the expected profits and losses in good time. With such information, you can easily delve into the trade with confidence knowing what you should expect from the market. By using the right trading styles and sticking to the right strategies, you can easily reduce losses and make the most out of each trading period.

In a nutshell, it is in order to say that options feature limited risks and unlimited profits.

When the cost of an option has not favored you by

the time of expiration, you can allow it to expire worthlessly, but you will lose your premium. This is why, just like any other form of investment, it is advisable that you only invest what you can afford to lose. The level of risk involved depends on your level of expertise and commitment. If you become careless in your trades, the risks may increase, and you may end up losing each time.

Chapter 9. Options Help You to Generate Passive Income

The options market involves the use of several strategies. Some of these strategies can help you generate some passive income from the trade. For instance, the covered call strategy allows you to purchase stock, then earn some cash selling calls from the same stock to investors. This way, you are still the owner of the stock, but making some returns from the stock at the same time.

Other strategies assist you in making maximum use of market factors such as volatility and time decay. Options spread and combination strategies also assist you in gaining more from the market. As you trade, you may keep growing your stock from the returns.

If you add more shares to a stock that pays dividends, you will be able to grow your income significantly.

Chapter 10. Options Provide Leverage for Your Investment

For each option contract that you start, you either purchase or sell 100shares of stock. This means that you can gain control over a large numberof shares without utilizing large amounts of capital.

This is because the amount you need to trade an option is far much less than the exact price of the shares.

By spending less on each contract, you will be able to enter more positions and trade in large amounts of underlying stocks within a shorter period of time. As a result, you will multiply your profits faster and this will translate faster growth of your investments.

Buying an options contract does not give you any right to the underlying shares. You only gain access to a small percentage of the underlying security.

If the other party decides to exercise the contract before expiration, there is very little and, in some cases, nothing to lose. Since the value of an option is affected by several other factors besides the value of the underlying asset, it is very easy to make good money from positions even atthe time that the cost of the underlying equity has not made any significant change. This explains the reason why the options market has both small as well as more established investors.

Options Offer More Flexibility and Versatility

Options trading is very flexible. This is one of the many factors that make investors flood the options market. The contracts always feature the most versatile terms and the strategies involved in the trade are quite diverse. Traders can comfortably apply a combination of strategies on a singlecontract to make the best in terms of capital.

Options are also bought and sold depending on a wide array of underlying assets.

asides understanding the direction, which prices may take, you can alsoget to find out how the prices of foreign currencies, indices, and commodities can change in the future. This helps you to know the type of underlying security you need to go for to ensure that you get quick profits.

With the many strategies in place, it becomes very easy to determine the kind of opportunities to invest in. For instance, if you are skilled in determining changes in the foreign exchange market, you can easily apply this skill in the options market to determine how the market is going to change over time. One great strategy that ensures flexibility of options trading is the use of spreads. You can significantly reduce the cost of trading by incorporating certain spreads and combinations. These not only reduce the risk of entering certain positions but also enable you to make a profit from price changes in more than one direction. In uncertain trades, you can use these strategies to hedge certain positions as a way of minimizing losses.

You may also use options to create synthetic trade positions, which offer you several opportunities that help you to attain your profit goals. These positions are commonly used by experts and provide a great alternative to the normal strategies used in options trading.

Flexibility in options trading is also enhanced by how

people use their time. When it comes to options, it is not a must for you to spend all day watching the market for you to gain profit. Options allow you to create your contracts based on predicted price movements. This is totally different from the buy and holds strategies used in other investment tools. If you invest in an option contract with a high probability of success, it is not a must that you spend time monitoring the trade. You can define stop-loss orders to ensure that a contract position closes as soon as the direction of the market changes.

Besides all this, you also have the opportunity to dictate the duration of each contract. You can, therefore, trade on a daily, weekly, monthly, or even annual basis depending on the amount of time you have. For instance, if you have more time within the day, you can take up daily positions.

The benefits listed above explain why options trading has been appealing to a good number of investors. The process is quite simple and a lot of profit can be made within a short time period. When you balance your contracts properly, you can easily reduce risks in your overall portfolio. For example, you may decide to combine selling stock and buying a put option at the same time. This will grant you an advantage when the stock price goes up, and limit losses in case of the stock price decreases. When coming up with a trading plan for the options market, you must beware of every aspect involved in the market. First, you must understand what account you need to be able to trade, as well as the amount of capital required as premium. With a good plan, you will be able to trade successfully and keep improving with time.

Conclusion

Hone your intuition: If you hope to be a successful day trader then you are going to need to get into the habit of making popular trades before they become popular for the best results. As such, you need to get into the habit of always following the beat of your own drum when it comes to drawing conclusions from your research and acting accordingly. While this doesn't mean listening to your gut, if you have put in the time and done the work and it all points in a direction that no one else has gone in yet then you need to be confident enough in your abilities to get in before things turn in that direction and you miss out on profits that were by all rights yours to lose. Knowing when to separate yourself from the pack is what separates average day traders from rich ones.

While this sounds relatively straightforward in theory, in practice, it is much more often about understanding when a certain trade is being hyped by those with something to gain and when the facts are actually pointing in a specific direction. While the most surefire way to learn the difference is through experience, eventually you will be able to determine the difference between a good trade and a good story and make money off the sheep who aren't aware there is a difference in the process. If you are having trouble believing in yourself in this way, then the best way to bolster your confidence is to start with listening to your intuition on smaller trades.

The success of any type will make it easier to trust yourself on more important trades in the future and should be celebrated appropriately to ensure they will be remembered the next time a similar situation arises. Remember, just because you are trading in short time frames doesn't mean you need to rush the decisions you make, only by fully thinking through every decision that you make will you know that you have truly made the right decision. A rash decision is a surefire way to lose money, no two ways around it.

Never let your losses build: As a new trader, it can be easy to become emotionally invested in the stocks you choose which is why it is crucial that you learn to separate your expectations for a trade from the reality of what occurs when the rubber meets the road. To successfully ensure that you don't lose more than the bare minimum on a given trade it is important that you cut its lose the second it stops generating a profit as opposed to hanging on to it in hopes that it turns around and rebounds in the correct direction.

It is important to learn early that a failed trade is not a reflection on you as a trader but simply a part of the natural trading process. Sticking with a losing trade is rarely, if ever, going to result in that trade turning around, and if it does the results are going to be middling at best. Likewise, it is never a good idea to double down on a losing trade as a means of mitigating a potential loss. Adding to a losing position is akin to trying to dig yourself out of a hole, it is never going to work no matter how hard you want it to.

Understand that sometimes the market simply has nothing to offer when many new traders get into the habit of buying up stocks, they feel as though they need to keep it up, even if the market isn't presenting anything worthwhile at the moment. It is important to understand that quality is going to supersede quantity every single time. Making changes to the stocks you are holding too often can easily decrease your profit margins and hurt your trading plan in the process as it will be difficult to determine just how effective you are actually being. Rather, it is always a better choice to simply let your current investments matriculate and wait until something that is actually better comes along before you do anything rash. Extra trades mean extra chances for loss, while poorly researched trades mean extra chances for loss as well. With these types of odds is it any wonder why these types of trades can quickly destroy all your profits?

Focus on yourself: If you are looking for a way to lose money while day trading, there will never be a more effective means of doing so than by trying to follow the trading plans that work for other people. A trading plan is an extremely personal expression of your goals for the market of your choice and the way that you are going to interact with it. As such, it requires plenty of trial and error, as well as personal introspection to ensure that it works with your natural trading tendencies as opposed to against them.

While looking at the level of success that professional traders have can make it difficult to forge your own path, mimicking what they are trying to do is only going to prove to be an exercise in futility ultimately. It is important to instead avoid the temptation by keeping in mind that knowing yourself and your strengths and weaknesses is the most reliable path to success.

Avoid trades that are out of the money: While there are a few strategies out there that make it a point of picking up options that are currently out of the money, you can rest assured that they are most certainly the exception, not the rule. Remember, the options market is not like the traditional stock market which means that even if you are trading options based on underlying stocks buying low and selling high is just not a viable strategy. If a call has dropped out of the money, there is generally less than a 10 percent chance that it will return to acceptable levels before it expires which means that if you purchase these types of options what you are doing is little better than gambling, and you can find ways to gamble with odds in your favor of much higher than 10 percent.

Always consider the source of tips: As a new day trader, you will likely be on the lookout for potential trading advice from anywhere and everywhere you can find it. This is a perfectly natural response to the magnitude of possible opportunities out there, and it can even be fruitful in the long run, but only if you know whose tips you should trust and whose you should take with a grain of salt. Many dubious tips start off from an honest place, someone you know who is talking about a company that is soon going to do something like releasing a new killer product, have groundbreaking earnings or who is going to be purchased by a major conglomerate.

Additionally, you will find many financial personalities on television touting this type of asset or that as the be all and end all of trading. While occasionally these types of tips will pay out, in general, the financial personality will have a stake in the investment, or it will turn out to just be the new fad for the next few months before it is forgotten entirely. This is not to say that you should avoid all trading tips entirely, rather it is to point out that before you go ahead and make a move you are going to want to do your own research on the investment and then move forward only if you feel the reasoning behind the investment is sound.